In the Land of Snake Charmers

A collection of poems

By
Moha

PRiSM Audio Visual International Inc.

ISBN: 978-0-6151-8902-4

Published by PRiSM AVI Inc.
Irvine, California.

About the Author

Moha came to America in June of 1988 from Bombay, India. Weaving her way through the challenges of coming to a new country, Moha has found great joy among children.
Now, she is committed towards creating better understanding between people of different cultures and religions. She lives in Irvine, California with her husband and two children.

A UNIQUE POETRY BOOK

This poetry book is unique because there is something different in it for you to do.

Write on "your page"
Write something about the poem. It is your page!

Draw on "your page"
Draw the pictures that come to mind while reading the poem.
Illustrate the poem.

The best part is that there is no *one* way to go about it. You can choose to interpret these poems in your own way.

For Ro-Pri
And
My friends, the children of the playground

"The more that you read, the more things you will know.
The more that you learn the more places you'll go."
-Dr. Seuss

In the Land of Snake Charmers

These poems are a collection of unique experiences of growing up "In the Land of Snake Charmers". Growing up in India is comprised of a variety of experiences. I want to share these experiences with the children of the world by telling a story in verse. The content of this poetry book expresses the flavor of growing up in India. It opens a window to children everywhere, transporting them into a world of adventures like "The Camel Ride" and riding in an "Auto Rickshaw". The children can sympathize with the street child who has "Nowhere to Go" and experience the messy job of eating "Mangoes".

I hope that while reading these poems, children can glimpse into the memories of childhood from another culture and find something they can relate to in their own culture.

In the Land of Snake Charmers

In the Land of Snake Charmers

Where tigers stalk in quiet solitude
Where peacocks parade their shimmering tails
Where villagers rouse to arduous days
Where scholars uphold their love for learning
Where poetry echoes through hill and dale
Where the scent of spices wafts through the air
Where music travels beyond boundaries
Where movies allow momentary dreams
Where heroic tales are narrated with flair
Where many religions come together
Where the mountains rise to meet the sky
Where freedom rang at the stroke of midnight
    This is the land I call my home
    This is the land I am free to roam

Your Page
Write and/or Draw
About
In the Land of Snake Charmers

Nowhere to Go

Nowhere to go
Aimlessly he roams
The street child
Has no home

Not much to eat
Forget about treats
He wanders alone
In the scorching heat

Strangers stare
Without a care
Stepping aside
With a lofty air

Day after day
This is the way
The street child
Learns to stay

Nowhere to go
Aimlessly he roams
The street child
Has no home

Your Page
Write and/or Draw
About
<u>Nowhere to Go</u>

Mangoes

Come not near
Better stay clear
When we eat
Mangoes here
Messy hands
Sticky face
Not a pretty sight
I fear
Golden, ripe,
Delicious, sweet,
Mangoes are
Such a treat!

Your Page
Write and/or Draw
About
Mangoes

Monkey Business

The leaves rustled
In the old fig tree
The meddling monkeys
Watched greedily

Leaping swiftly
Without a fear
Snatching food
From anyone near

Startled little girls
Losing their poise
Hiding their fear
Scared little boys

Again and again
The monkeys strike
Snatching all kinds
Of foods they like

The meddling monkeys
Must be blocked
This monkey business
Must be stopped

Your Page
Write and/or Draw
About
Monkey Business

The Schoolmaster

The clock strikes nine
The stern schoolmaster
Wearing a faint smile
Arrives exactly on time

Good Morning Sir
In chorus we greet
Good Morning children
You may take your seats

Creaking chairs
Open books
Backpacks hanging
On tired hooks

The schoolmaster
Begins with a frown
Today's lesson
Is all about nouns

Your Page
Write and/or Draw
About
__The Schoolmaster__

The Marketplace

Come one! Come all!
Won't you buy from my stall?
Big brown potatoes
Shiny red tomatoes
Long string beans
Chillies so green
Bright yellow lemons
Big round melons
Sweet juicy peaches
Delicious lychees
Come one! Come all!
Won't you buy from my stall?

Your Page
Write and/or Draw
About
The Marketplace

Juhu Beach

Juhu Beach is a hop, skip and jump away
From the place where I stay
Young and old
Come to stroll
Munch on snacks
Sold on racks
Muddy trails
Deck the sand
Horse and carriage
Looking grand
Little hands
Shaping dreams
Feasting on
Icy cream
Radiant mornings
Dusky evenings
Another day
Folds away
Juhu Beach is a hop, skip and jump away
From the place where I stay

Your Page
Write and/or Draw
About
Juhu Beach

The Camel Ride

Do you fancy?
A camel ride

Hop right on
The camel's back

Feel the jiggle
Without fear

Hold on tight
While you wiggle

Feast your eyes
On the sights

Journey along
The bumpy ride

Leaning forward
With a jolt

The camel drops
On bended knees

Safe and sound
On the ground

Slide right off
The camel's back

Did you enjoy
The camel ride?

Your Page
Write and/or Draw
About
The Camel Ride

Mosquitoes

Buzzing around
Here and there
Pesky mosquitoes
Are everywhere

Circling around
In steady flight
They are poised
To aim and strike

Hopping around
On my toes
Ready to dodge
Those itchy bites

Buzzing around
Here comes one
Landing boldly
On my knee

Splat!

Your Page
Write and/or Draw
About
Mosquitoes

No School Today

It's raining
It's pouring
I'm not complaining
There's no school today!

Heavy rains
Cancelled trains
Flooded streets
Splashing feet
Stomping away
With steady beat

Stranded cars
Can't get far
People grumbling
Some are mumbling
No one seems
To be enjoying

It's raining
It's pouring
I'm not complaining
There's no school today!

Your Page
Write and/or Draw
About
No School Today

231 Limited

The rumble of the big red bus
Can be heard from a distance
Passengers fret as they wait
The double decker is a little late
Welcome aboard the 231 Limited!
Some dash up the spiral stairs
Others linger in the passageway
The conductor calls, "Tickets please!"
Passengers fumble, looking for change
Some are in for a long ride
Others exit with a quick stride
Markets, schools and railway stations
The stops come in quick succession
Watch your step as you get off
Thank you for your patronage!

Your Page
Write and/or Draw
About
231 Limited

Paper Kites

The sky is full of colorful kites
As onlookers gaze in sheer delight

Like diamonds dancing in the sky
The paper kites are flying high

Then it happens for all to see
The dancing diamond gets caught in a tree

A hush falls upon the crowd
As it tumbles to the ground

Dismal looks turn to smiles
When another kite soars with might

Your Page
Write and/or Draw
About
Paper Kites

Diwali

Tune in to the echoes of merriment
You will hear the jingle of bangles
The crisp rustle of organza gowns

Glance around the cityscapes
You will see an array of lights
Glittering in the darkness of night

Taste the flavors of the festival
You will relish the delicious treats
Sweetmeats prepared for the feast

Feel the spirit of brotherhood
You will treasure the loyalty
Sharing a legacy of ancient history

Savor this splendid night
It is the night when we celebrate
Diwali, festival of lights

Your Page
Write and/or Draw
About
Diwali

The Auto Rickshaw

Look! There it goes

The odd-looking rickshaw

Have you seen it before?

With three wheels, not four

One small hood and zero doors

The rickshaw takes off with a roar!

The driver steers from his seat

Passengers huddle with dangling feet

Be prepared to feel the bumps

When the auto rickshaw jumps

In and out it zooms about

As it speeds noisily!

The auto rickshaw with three wheels
Not four…

Is truly quite a discovery!

Your Page
Write and/or Draw
About
The Auto Rickshaw

The Village Boy

Racing barefoot
In the sun
The village boy
Is having fun
In his hands
He holds a stick
A stick to tap
A worn out wheel
As it rolls
With just one tap
The village boy
Runs with joy

The worn-out wheel
Keeps on rolling
Until it stops
Like a twirling top
One last time
He taps the wheel
Freedom digging
At his heels
As it rolls
With just one tap
The village boy
Runs with joy

Your Page
Write and/or Draw
About
The Village Boy

Off To School

Rahul and Rima ride their bikes
Dolly never fails to hike

Raj has a chauffeured ride
The car is his father's pride

Priya has to take the bus
Just like so many of us

Maya rides with her own dad
In a yellow and black taxi cab

Jai is ready for the bumps
When the auto rickshaw jumps

That leaves Somu, the village boy
Who is off to a very slow start
On Uncle Swami's bullock cart

Your Page
Write and/or Draw
About
Off To School

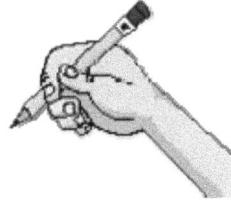

The Traffic Relay

The big red bus looms over the wide open truck

The wide open rickety truck pushes into the rotund van

The rotund old clunky van edges into the stylish car

The stylish little sporty car zooms ahead of the taxi cab

The yellow and black taxi cab vrooms into the auto rickshaw

The odd looking auto rickshaw blocks the rugged motorbike

The well-built motorbike closes into the feathery bicycle

The feather-light bicycle almost runs over the man on foot

The grumpy man on foot scowls as he boards the big red bus

The big red bus looms over the wide open truck…

Your Page
Write and/or Draw
About
The Traffic Relay

Mahatma Gandhi

One little man
Short and thin
Believed strongly
That lying was a sin

One little man
With round glasses
Believed in equality
For people of all classes

One little man
Simply clad
Believed in the freedom
Of one's own land

One little man
A great big soul
Believed in non-violence
For one and all

Your Page
Write and/or Draw
About
Mahatma Gandhi

Special thanks to Rohan Mehta for formatting and editing.

Special thanks to Priyanka Mehta for designing the covers.

Rohan's favorite poem:
"if everything happens that can't be done"- E. E. Cummings

Priyanka's favorite poems:
"The Raven"- Edgar Allen Poe
"Out, Out"- by Robert Frost

These are a few of my favorite poems.

"Where the Mind Is Without Fear"- Rabindranath Tagore

"The Road Not Taken"- Robert Frost
"Stopping by the Woods on a Snowy Evening"- Robert Frost
"Mending Wall"- Robert Frost

"Tyger Tyger"- William Blake

"O Captain! My Captain!"- Walt Whitman

"Life Doesn't Frighten Me"- Maya Angelou

"Lochinvar"- Sir Walter Scott

"The Highwayman"-Alfred Noyes

<u>Note to children and adults:</u>
There are many more wonderful poems to lift the spirit. Explore websites and books under the guidance of your parents.

Glossary

All word meanings obtained from Merriam Webster Online:
http://www.m-w.com/

Auto-rickshaw---A three-wheeled vehicle

Bangles---an ornamental disk that hangs loosely (as on a bracelet)

Bullock-cart---a wagon pulled by bulls or oxen, usually a form of transportation in India's villages

Chauffeur--- a person employed to drive a motor vehicle

Dale---valley

Diwali---A festival celebrated in India

Double Decker---something that is double (231 limited is a double decker bus)

Juhu Beach---A real beach in Mumbai, India

Non-violence- Free from violence as a principle

Organza--- a sheer dress fabric (as of silk or nylon)

Snake charmer---an entertainer who exhibits a professed power to charm or fascinate venomous snakes

Stall---a booth, stand, or counter at which articles are displayed for sale

Sweetmeats---foods rich in sugar, usually a dessert.

Taxicab-an automobile that carries passengers for a fare usually determined by the distance traveled

Dedications

This book is dedicated to my mummy and papa, Raksha and Parry Dholakia, my husband Sushrut, my brother Rahul, and my children Rohan and Priyanka.

Dakshesh Maama   *Akshu maasa*

Pritiba   *Plaza Vista Family*

I would also like to thank my circle of family and friends. Thanks for your love and support!

Bombay
Those were the days...

www.ingramcontent.com/pod-product-compliance
Lightning Source LLC
LaVergne TN
LVHW061340060426
835511LV00014B/2035